THE
GHOSTLY TALES
OF
NEW
ENGLAND

Published by Arcadia Children's Books
A Division of Arcadia Publishing
Charleston, SC
www.arcadiapublishing.com

Spooky America is a trademark of Arcadia Publishing, Inc.

First published 2020

Manufactured in the United States

ISBN 978-1-4671-9806-6
Library of Congress Control Number: 2020938911

Photo credits: used throughout Eugenia Petrovskaya/Shutterstock.com; p. iv-v, 4, 28, 42, 60, 76, 88 The Hornbills Studio/Shutterstock.com, Caso Alfonso/ Shutterstock.com, Ivakoleva/Shutterstock.com, LDDesign/Shutterstock.com; p. vi Jordan Delmonte/Shutterstock.com; p. 3 KsanaGraphica/Shutterstock.com; p. 8, 98 Cattallina/Shutterstock.com; p. 18-19 Adam Gladstone/Shutterstock.com; p. 24, 33, 70, 92 vectorkuro/Shutterstock.com; p. 38-39 Songquan Deng/Shutterstock.com; p. 49 Stock2You/Shutterstock.com; p. 54-55 Christopher Georgia/Shutterstock.com; p. 83 Forgem/Shutterstock.com; p. 87 4kclips/Shutterstock.com; p. 104 Ihnatovich Maryia/ Shutterstock.com.

Spooky America

THE
GHOSTLY TALES
OF
NEW
ENGLAND

CARIE JUETTNER

Adapted from *A Guide to Haunted New England* by Thomas D'Agostino

ARCADIA
PUBLISHING

MAINE

VERMONT

7
8
6

11
9
10

14
13
16
15

NEW
HAMSPHIRE

12

ATLANTIC OCEAN

3
4
1
5
2

MASSACHUSETTS

CONNECTICUT

17
18
19

21
22
20

RHODE ISLAND

Table of Contents & Map Key

Introduction

New England is a fascinating part of the United States. This is where the Pilgrims landed, where Paul Revere made his midnight ride, and where generations of immigrants have started new lives in America. This is where you can ski, hit the beach, see the gorgeous fall leaves, and meet beautiful wildlife on thousands of miles of hiking trails. But do you know what else New England is famous for? GHOSTS. Hundreds of years of history—and millions of residents over those years—mean there are lots of dead and buried folk. But some of the dead aren't ready to leave yet.

Yankee *spirits* are alive and well in this collection of New England ghost stories. A mad doctor who kidnaps children? A headless woman who haunts a chasm? Phantom pirates who wander the shore? You'll meet them all within these pages. So find a comfy spot and settle in for some tales of terror, but don't get *too* comfortable. Stay alert, and look behind you once in a while, because these ghost stories are *true*.

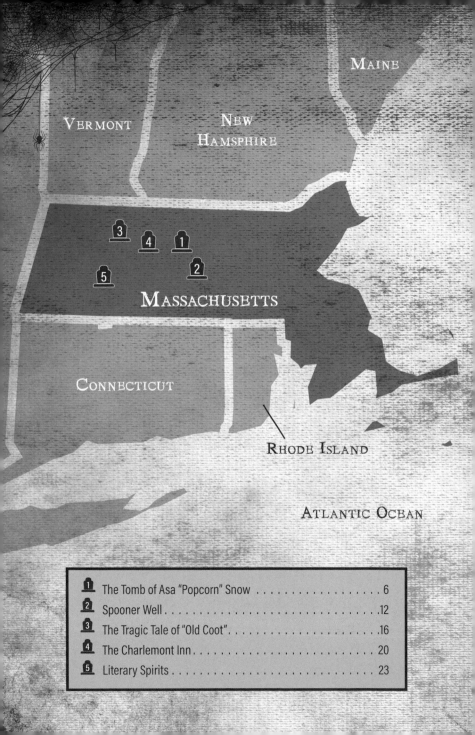

MAINE

VERMONT

NEW
HAMSPHIRE

MASSACHUSETTS

CONNECTICUT

RHODE ISLAND

ATLANTIC OCEAN

Massachusetts

The Boston Tea Party, Plymouth Rock, the Freedom Trail, the USS *Constitution*, the Salem Witch Trials, Paul Revere, and the Shot Heard 'Round the World. Some call Massachusetts the "birthplace of the nation," and it's easy to see why. There is so much history here, so much American pride mixed with so much hardship. This is the same state where a brave man made a midnight ride to warn the community that the British were coming, and where a village sentenced innocent young women to death for witchcraft. It is a state full of history, and mystery, and ghosts. Let us introduce you to a few of them.

CHAPTER 1

The Tomb of Asa "Popcorn" Snow

If you're looking for a weird story with a bizarre main character and unexpected twists, look no further than the tale of Asa "Popcorn" Snow.

Asa Snow was born in the 1790s in Cape Cod, Massachusetts, but in 1840, he moved to Dana, in Worcester County. The town of Dana no longer exists. In the 1930s, the county created the Quabbin Reservoir, right where Dana sat. That meant that all the houses and buildings in Dana had to be moved or demolished to make way for the river to flood the land. Imagine having to give up your home to make room for an artificial lake! Even the graves had to be relocated. This was a grisly task. More than seven *thousand* bodies had to be dug up, moved, and reburied. Today, in the part of Dana that is still above water, only cellars and walls remain. A monument dedicated to the people who sacrificed their homes marks the place where the town commons used to be.

But for Asa Snow, that was still ninety years away. Asa settled in to Dana and quickly earned the nickname "Popcorn" because of his strange diet. He ate mostly popcorn and milk.

Popcorn had strange ideas about death and how the deceased should be mourned. His tragic life gave him plenty of opportunities to demonstrate this fascination. When his first wife, Isabelle, took her own life in their barn, Asa displayed her dead body and invited anyone who wished to come see her. Then he buried her. When their daughter died a year later, he buried her next to her mother. However, twenty years later, Popcorn built a family vault in his own backyard. He dug up the bodies of his wife and daughter and moved them there.

As Popcorn grew older, he became obsessed with thoughts of his own passing and began planning for his death. He started making himself a coffin. Instead of building it out of wood, he made a metal casket with a glass top. He also made the undertaker promise that, when Popcorn died, the man would spend seven days watching over his body in the glass coffin, just in case he woke up. The man reluctantly agreed.

On November 29, 1872, Popcorn was dragging the

body of a slaughtered pig into his house. He was going to make dinner for guests when he suddenly dropped dead. His body was laid out in the metal coffin and placed inside the family crypt. The loyal undertaker followed Asa's orders, checking in on him every day. However, after three days of monitoring the body, Asa's second wife told the man he could go, and the tomb was closed.

Asa Popcorn Snow's strange story does not end with his death. The rumors of Asa's peculiar characteristics and unique coffin spread, making him a legend in Dana and beyond. People were curious about his body. What did it look like beneath the glass? In 1912—*forty years* after Popcorn's death—a reporter decided to find out. He opened the Snow family vault and looked inside. His verdict? It was uncanny how well Asa's body had held up after all that time! His hair had not lost its color and his clothes were still like new.

The report also mentioned another odd fact. After Asa's death, the remains of his first wife, Isabelle, and his daughter had been placed in a box on top of his coffin. However, rumor has it, someone stole Isabelle's teeth from her skull and used them to decorate a timepiece. Why anyone would want a clock made of human teeth is unknown, but that is what the legend claims.

Eventually, someone snuck into the vault and broke the glass on Asa's coffin. The effect was immediate and ghastly. Exposed to the elements, Popcorn's body decomposed rapidly until it was too gruesome to be viewed. After this, the tomb was sealed permanently. Then, when the reservoir was created, the bodies of Asa and his family were relocated and buried in the Quabbin Park Cemetery with the rest of the town of Dana.

It may not surprise you to learn that a man so obsessed with death does not rest peacefully in his tomb. Each November, the ghost of Asa leaves his grave to visit the world he used to inhabit. The glowing form has been known to float around the ruins of his old home and to visit the original grave of his first wife.

If you find yourself in the vicinity of the old town of Dana on a November evening, keep an eye out for Asa "Popcorn" Snow.

Spooner Well

Locals say that Spooner Well in Brookfield, Massachusetts, is haunted. Once you know the history of the site, you'll understand why.

Joshua and Bathsheba Spooner lived in Brookfield in the late 1700s, but they did not have a happy marriage. Joshua was an abusive alcoholic, and Bathsheba wanted to be free of him. Then, in 1777, she took in a young soldier, weary and ill, whom she met on his way back from fighting in George Washington's army.

His name was Ezra Ross, and he was only sixteen years old. Bathsheba nursed Ezra back to health and, despite his young age, the two of them fell in love. After Ezra was healed, he went back home to Linbrook, but he and Mrs. Spooner kept in touch.

Now that she loved Ezra, Bathsheba had another reason for wanting her husband gone. So when two British soldiers—James Buchanan and William Brooks—became lodgers at her house, she hatched a plan to get rid of Joshua *permanently*. She wrote to Ezra telling him to hurry back, that she had arranged for a way they could be together. Her plan? She wanted Brooks and Buchanan to kill her husband. The two men were hesitant at first, but Bathsheba convinced them with tales of Joshua's wickedness and by promising to pay them.

On March 1, 1778, they put their plan into action. It was William Brooks who did the terrible deed. He hid behind the gate while Joshua Spooner was visiting Cooley's Tavern. When Joshua headed home, William jumped him, beating and strangling the startled man until he breathed no more. Then James Buchanan and Ezra Ross helped throw Joshua's body into the Spooners' well.

Bathsheba's wicked plan had worked. She was free of her husband forever.

Satisfied, she paid the men and sent them on their way. However, in her joy at pulling off her husband's killing, she made a fatal mistake. Not realizing what she was doing, Bathsheba sent a servant to the well for water. There, Mr. Spooner's body was discovered.

Witnesses who had seen the British soldiers lodging at the Spooner house told the authorities, and they were quickly arrested, along with Ezra. But the men wasted no time in pointing the finger of blame at Bathsheba, saying that she was the instigator of the crime. The trial took place on April 24, 1778, and lasted all day, from eight in the morning until midnight. In the end, all four were convicted of murder and sentenced to death by hanging.

Bathsheba claimed that she was pregnant and begged for a stay of execution until she delivered her baby. But the midwives who examined her gave conflicting opinions on her condition. With no proof of her pregnancy, she was executed with the men. Bathsheba Spooner became the first woman hanged in the new American Republic.

So whose spirit haunts the Spooner Well? Is it the ghost of Joshua Spooner, who met his end there, murdered by the will of his wife? Or is it Bathsheba herself, finally feeling remorseful for her heinous act? Why not visit yourself and find out?

The Tragic Tale of "Old Coot"

In the 1860s, Massachusetts sent many young men—fathers, sons, husbands, brothers—to fight in the Civil War. One of those young men was William Saunders.

William left his family to fight for the Union army in 1861. A year later, his wife, Belle, received the upsetting news that her husband had been seriously injured in battle. Belle was distraught. When months passed and no more news arrived, she feared her beloved William had died of his wounds.

Still grieving her husband, Belle hired a man to help her work on her farm. They grew close and eventually married. The man even adopted her children.

In 1865, the war ended, and the surviving soldiers returned home. One of them was William Saunders. William had miraculously survived his wounds, but the war had changed him. Though he had been gone only four years, he looked much older. His scraggly beard, ragged appearance, and the scars from his injuries made him unrecognizable to the people he once knew.

Even his wife.

When he saw Belle happily living with another man, and when he heard his children call that man "Daddy," poor William's heart broke. He left town and built himself a small cabin at Mount Greylock, near what is now the Bellows Pipe Trail.

William lived the rest of his life there, doing odd jobs for the locals, sometimes even working for his wife and her new husband, but no one called him by his name again. When asked, he wouldn't give a name, so people started calling him "Old Coot." Some said he was insane, others pitied him for what the war had done to him, but everyone pretty much left Old Coot alone. Then, one freezing day in the heart of winter, some hunters stumbled upon Old Coot's shack.

Inside, they found the old soldier dead.

While the hunters were staring at the sad sight, wondering what to do, Old Coot's spirit leaped from his body! The hunters jumped back in alarm as the specter of Old Coot tore out of the cabin and scurried up the mountain.

Ever since that day, countless witnesses have seen Old Coot's ghost on Mount Greylock. He is always seen running up the mountain, never down. It seems poor William is still trying to escape the tragedies of his life. Maybe one day, his spirit will finally be free.

CHAPTER 4

The Charlemont Inn

Built in 1787, the Charlemont Inn has seen its share of history, famous guests, and paranormal activity. President Calvin Coolidge, General John Burgoyne, famous author Mark Twain, and famous traitor Benedict Arnold all stayed at the inn at one time or another. Those men came and went, but some guests have remained eternally at this haunted hotel.

Stay in room 23, and you may have the privilege of meeting Elizabeth, the ghost of a young woman who favors that space. Elizabeth is not a quiet guest. If you hear the clatter of high heel shoes or the creak of someone ascending the staircase (when no one is in sight), you've probably encountered Elizabeth. She's a messy ghost too. She often leaves the bed covers in disarray and has been known to move things around in room 23.

Another spirit that haunts the Charlemont Inn is the ghost of a Revolutionary War soldier. Some speculate that it might be Ephraim Brown, the man who built the inn. However, neither Elizabeth nor the soldier seem to be to blame for one of the eeriest things that ever happened in the parlor.

A large mirror used to hang on the wall in the parlor of the Charlemont Inn in what appears to be a powerful spot for otherworldly activity. Paranormal investigators once photographed the room and noticed three vortexes, or cross-points in energy fields, near the location of the mirror. (These energy vortexes are where experts think spirits can travel between worlds.) Perhaps that has something to do with the fact that one day the mirror was discovered on the floor across the room from where it once hung. The glass had been shattered, but each tiny fragment was still in its proper place, forming the shape of the mirror. No one on the premises had heard a sound.

Sadly, this historic haunt now sits empty and unused. However, some local residents are trying to save it from demolition. If they succeed, the ghosts of the Charlemont Inn will have the chance to "live" another day.

CHAPTER 5

Literary Spirits

New England has been home to many famous authors and poets. The houses of Mark Twain and Harriet Beecher Stowe sit side by side in Hartford, Connecticut. Emily Dickinson grew up in Amherst, Massachusetts, and Robert Frost made his home in New Hampshire. Stephen King still lives in Bangor, Maine. Nathaniel Hawthorne was born in Salem, Massachusetts, and later lived in various places across New England. He is buried in the Sleepy Hollow Cemetery in Concord, Massachusetts, along with Louisa May Alcott, Ralph Waldo Emerson, and Henry David Thoreau. Admirers of these influential writers leave pens and pencils and thank you notes on their graves, showing how much they are still loved despite how long it's been since they walked the earth.

One famous author who is *not* buried in New England but has strong ties there—especially in Massachusetts—is Edith Wharton. Wharton was born in New York. When her family was not traveling in Europe, they split their time between New York and Newport, Rhode Island. Later, after she married, Wharton and her husband moved to The Mount in Lenox, Massachusetts. The author designed the beautiful country estate herself. Although she and her husband only lived there for a few years, she loved the house and considered it her "first real home."

When Edith Wharton died in 1937, her body was laid to rest in France, but The Mount still stands, and some say that's where her spirit resides, and it's not alone. The ghost of Henry James, another famous writer and good friend of Wharton, also haunts the place. Based on the strange sights and sounds that have been reported, other specters may dwell there as well.

After the Whartons left The Mount, it became the Fox Hollow Boarding School and then later the home of the Shakespeare and Company theater troupe. The actors that resided in the mansion reported all sorts of unexplained noises, such as typewriters tapping and schoolgirls giggling. Some even glimpsed the apparition of Edith Wharton roaming the halls and Henry James standing in the room where he used to stay when he visited. But even those uncanny accounts can't compare to what Andrea Haring witnessed in The Mount one day.

Andrea, a voice teacher for the theater company, was taking a nap in Edith Wharton's room. When she awoke, the room that had been warm when she entered was freezing cold. And when she opened her eyes, she was shocked to see that everything looked different. Antique furniture adorned the room, which had been mostly empty before. Andrea was still taking in this strange sight when she noticed three people in the corner of the room. The spirit of Edith Wharton lounged on a sofa, while the figure of her husband stood nearby. A second man (perhaps Henry James?) was seated at a desk. The man at the desk was writing something, and all three of them were engaged in lively conversation, but no sound issued forth.

Stunned by this surreal scene from another world, Andrea stood and started for the door. All three figures froze and stared right at her. Not knowing what else to do, the frightened young woman nodded at the trio, and they returned the gesture. Having left the room, Andrea rushed to find her friends and tell them what she'd seen, but when they returned to the room, the chill had dissipated, the ghosts were gone, and the furniture was as it should be again.

It has been said that writers live forever through their books and stories, but it seems that some authors are not satisfied with that type of immortality. Some choose to linger in this realm in a more substantial way.

VERMONT

MASSACHUSETTS

Vermont

Green mountains, snowy ski slopes, breathtaking fall foliage, and maple syrup. It's hard to imagine a more inviting combination. From Lake Champlain to the home of Ben & Jerry's Ice Cream, from its one hundred covered bridges to its innumerable hiking trails, Vermont appeals to nature lovers and families. But there is a darker side to this beautiful state. The restaurants attract creepy customers, the lake has a monster, and the university houses hordes of ghosts. Even the ice cream factory has a graveyard. So enjoy your time in this picturesque state, but always be on the lookout for unexpected visitors.

CHAPTER 6

The Monster of Lake Champlain

Most people have heard of the famous Loch Ness Monster in Scotland, but New England has its own mysterious creature of the deep that's been around even longer.

Between Vermont and New York stretches Lake Champlain, which is 125 miles long and up to four hundred feet deep in some places. Within those depths lurks "Champ," whose tales travel back more than four hundred years.

No one knows exactly what Champ is, but

there have been more than three hundred reports of her. The first dates all the way back to 1609, when Samuel de Champlain (yup, he's the guy the lake is named after) saw members of the Iroquois tribe battling with the strange creature on the riverbank. Champ must have survived that encounter with the Native Americans because the sightings continued.

In the late 1800s, Sheriff Nathan H. Mooney described Champ as being twenty-five to fifty feet long. That's as long as a train car! When P.T. Barnum heard this, he offered a reward of $50,000 for the capture of Champ so he could display her in his famous zoo. But Champ refused to be caught.

Fishermen, tourists, and ship captains continued to spot Champ from time to time, but in 1977, she was finally captured . . . in a photograph. Sandra Mansi took a picture of a long, slender, curving neck rising from the surface of the lake followed by what appears to be a beast's humped back. When Joseph Zarzynski, founder of the Lake Champlain Phenomena Investigation, saw the photograph, he admitted that it didn't look like any known lake animal. However, his investigations led to no further evidence of the creature in the picture.

Champ made her most public appearance on July 30, 1984. She emerged near a boat called *Spirit of Ethan Allen*, which was hosting a family party. The crowd watched in awe as the thirty-foot creature swam parallel to their boat, displaying five humps above the waves. She kept pace with them until an approaching speedboat scared her away.

Can you imagine having a guest like *that* at your party?

There have been many theories about what Champ *really* is. Some people think she could be a plesiosaurus, a prehistoric fish that existed during the Cretaceous period. Others believe Champ could be a longnose gar, a type of large fish with a long snout and sharp teeth. After Joseph Zarzynski's research led nowhere, he decided the "monster" in Sandra Mansi's photo could have been a log or tree branch.

But maybe the mystery can't be solved that easily. Despite what appeared in Sandra's picture, one thing is for sure: *something* lurks beneath the water of Lake Champlain. Is it an immortal river monster? The offspring of a long-lost dinosaur? Or something else? Take the ferry from Burlington, Vermont, to Port Kent, New York, and have a look for yourself. Maybe you'll catch a glimpse of Champ.

Chills at the Ice House

After visiting Lake Champlain and hanging out with Champ, people enjoy spending some time in Burlington, Vermont. A favorite place to grab a bite to eat used to be the Ice House. Unfortunately, the Ice House closed in 2016, but its eeriness left a big impression on its customers.

The popular eating establishment was once an actual icehouse. Before refrigeration, people used to cut large blocks of ice from frozen lakes and rivers in the winter and store them in icehouses—cold, insulated locations—so customers could have ice during the summer. The Ice House restaurant kept some of the same architecture of the original building and some of its memories too.

The cooks and staff at the Ice House frequently used to hear the scraping, dragging sound of large blocks of ice being moved across the floor and even ran into spirits and ghosts in the corridors and back rooms of the building. A chef named Justin was cleaning up in the kitchen one day when something caught his attention. He turned and saw an old woman swinging a bell. Justin blinked and noticed that he could see through the woman, and her bell made no sound. That's when he realized he was looking at a ghost! Unafraid, Justin took a step toward the apparition, but as he got closer, she vanished.

It was also hard to keep up with your belongings at the Ice House. Objects would move around on their own, disappearing from the place they were last seen and appearing later in strange, out-of-the-way locations. So it was unwise to leave your sunglasses unattended unless you wanted to hunt for them later.

Why did the Ice House have so many ghosts? The answer may stem from the building's original purpose. Working with ice was dangerous, and workers were often injured or even killed. The blocks were enormous, extremely heavy, and not easy to manage. Workers could fall into the frigid lakes where the ice was collected or fall victim to the enormous, sharp ice saws. And once in the icehouse, the huge blocks were piled in tall stacks. The blocks were known to slip out of place and fall, often crushing the men below. How many men died at the original icehouse in Vermont? That number is lost to history. But the souls that lingered clearly wanted us to remember them. Thanks to the Ice House restaurant, we will.

A School With a Lot of Spirit(s)

Would you want to attend a haunted college? If so, you may want to apply to the University of Vermont, where more than just students walk the dormitory halls.

The University of Vermont is more often referred to as UVM, which stands for *Universitas Viridis Montis* and means "University of Green Mountains." Several famous people have graduated from UVM, including John Dewey, creator of the Dewey Decimal System. But it's the students who decided to stay *forever* who are the most intriguing. The university was founded in 1791, so there's a lot of history there, and more than a few ghosts. *Fourteen* of the buildings are reportedly haunted!

Three places on the UVM campus where you're likely to run into a school *spirit* are Converse Hall, the Counseling Center, and the Public Relations building.

Converse Hall is breathtaking. Its Gothic style, pointed arches, and striking appearance make it seem more like the setting of a vampire movie than a college dorm. Every year, more than a hundred UVM students call this building home. One resident, though, isn't on the roster. His name is Henry, and he's been haunting Converse Hall for a hundred years.

Henry was a medical student at the University of Vermont in the 1920s. Sadly, he took his own life while he was there . . . and then decided to stay. At Converse Hall, doors open and close themselves, lights flicker at all hours, furniture rearranges itself when no one is looking, and small objects sometimes fly across the room on their own. It's common knowledge that this is all Henry's doing.

Once a student was alone in her room in Converse Hall when she heard *clickety-clack, clickety-clack.* It sounded like a typewriter. She left her room in search of the noise— *clickety-clack, clickety-clack*—but found no one typing. She even peered into the study room, where students used typewriters to complete their assignments. But all the desks were empty. The event scared her so much, the poor girl fled the building in a panic. Maybe it was Henry, still working hard on his medical degree.

Students visit UVM's Counseling Center seeking guidance and comfort, but what they sometimes find is an angry ghost with thick sideburns and a large round nose. People suspect this is the spirit of Captain John Nabb, the original owner of the old mansion where the counseling offices are located. Nabb is not a quiet ghost. He slams windows and doors, turns lights on and off, and once knocked over a custodian's mop bucket for no reason. No one knows what the ghost is so upset about, but it certainly seems like the captain is in need of some counseling!

The Public Relations building at UVM is also not as welcoming as it should be. If you try to enter one of the rooms here, you're likely to find the door . . . stuck. You push again. No luck. You try pulling. Nope. The door isn't locked, it just won't budge. You try one more time, and . . . finally! You're through. Sources say you've been a victim of the ghost of John E. Booth, the original owner of the house that now contains the Public Relations offices. He likes to hold doors closed on people while they try to open them and bangs around the building making noise and playing with the lights. What a trickster!

As you can see, if you choose to study at the University of Vermont, you'll have plenty of company and lots of interesting personalities to keep you on your toes.

MAINE

VERMONT

NEW
HAMSPHIRE

New Hampshire

New Hampshire's motto is "Live free or die," but some who die in this scenic state return to the land of the living. Among its cozy inns, charming farms, beautiful White Mountains, and thriving tourist scene, this state has some spooky secrets. Read on, and we'll let you in on a few of them.

The Ghost of Mount Washington

Imagine . . . it is a beautiful late-summer afternoon, and you are staying in the Glen House, a lodge at the base of scenic Mount Washington. At 2:00 p.m., you and your uncle and cousin decide to hike the trail up to Tip Top House at the mountain's summit.

The walk is farther than you thought. As you climb higher and higher, the sun sets lower and lower. Soon darkness falls, and a vicious, cold wind strikes. Unable to see or know how far you are from your destination, you and your companions take shelter behind some rocks. It is not enough protection. The wind seeps in, chilling you to the bone. Your heart races from fear, cold, and exhaustion until finally . . . it gives out. You breathe your last on the side of the mountain in the unforgiving elements.

The next morning, your grieving relatives awake to find they were only a few hundred yards from the summit, and safety.

This ghastly event happened on September 14, 1855, to twenty-three-year-old Lizzie Bourne. She and her cousin Lucy and her uncle George set out for the top of Mount Washington, unaware that nightfall, weather, and Lizzie's heart condition would be a deadly and tragic combination.

Poor Lizzie was buried in Kennebunk, Maine, but a grave marker rests next to the place where she died on Mount Washington. According to witnesses, Lizzie still visits the spot every year on the anniversary of her death. Those brave enough to venture close to the monument on September 14 report seeing a glowing, misty figure rise from the rocks where Lizzie died and float around her gravestone before forlornly dissolving into the shadows for another year.

The Mad Doctor of Mount Moosilauke

For centuries, people have been searching for the secret of eternal youth. Some say a doctor in the White Mountains may have found it.

Thomas Benton was born in the early 1800s. He studied medicine in Germany, then moved back to New Hampshire to become the first and only doctor in his town at the base of the White Mountains. Coincidentally, the town where he lived was called Benton. (It wasn't named for the young doctor, though. It was named for a

Missouri senator with the same name: Thomas Hart Benton).

Dr. Benton didn't just want to heal people; he wanted to find a way to keep them young forever. In his spare time, he did mysterious experiments, trying to create an elixir of youth. But playing with nature is a dangerous game, and Benton's ambition may have led to his later misfortunes.

Young Dr. Benton fell in love, but tragedy struck. Before the wedding, his bride-to-be got very sick and died. This drove the young doctor mad. He disappeared from the community, locking himself away in a cabin he built at the top of Mount Moosilauke.

That's when strange things began to happen.

First, farm animals started dying. But no one could determine the cause of death. The only sign of injury was a strange red swelling with a white pinprick on the animal's left ear. No one could explain it. No predator was known to leave such a mark. The farmers wondered if the mad doctor was doing experiments on their livestock and decided to visit his cabin. When they arrived, they found strange equipment and signs of weird experiments but no doctor. The man was nowhere to be seen.

What sorts of experiments was the mad doctor doing? What was the apparatus they found? We'll never know for sure. All we can be certain of is that the state of the doctor's cabin unnerved the men who explored it.

On the way back down the mountain, one farmer got separated from the group. His friends continued walking, assuming he'd catch up. He never did. Later, he was found dead, with a red swelling and a white pinprick behind his left ear.

Cattle continued to die with no explanation. The local farmers were getting more and more anxious. Then an even more monstrous mystery occurred: in nearby towns, babies began disappearing from their beds during the night. Now the villagers were truly frightened.

Then, one day, a woman was working in her yard with her daughter when a man with long white hair wearing a black cloak swooped out of the woods. He grabbed the young girl and carried her away as she screamed. The girl's father and a group of other men quickly chased the kidnapper, tracking his footprints to a high cliff. There, they found Dr. Benton holding his captive at the edge of the rock face.

"Release her!" the girl's father shouted.

Then the men watched in horror as the doctor did as they asked. He released the young girl, sending her tumbling to her death over the side of the mountain.

The doctor was never seen again. But mysterious events kept occurring in the White Mountains.

In 1860, thirty years after Dr. Benton was last seen, a hotel was built at the top of Mount Moosilauke. When a cable that helped hold the building in place was cut, a logger offered to climb up and fix it. He never returned. Later, he was found dead with—you guessed it—a red swelling and a white pinprick behind his left ear.

To this day, people often report seeing a dark, cloaked form roaming through the woods atop Mount Moosilauke at night. But the question remains, did the mad doctor discover the secret of eternal youth after all? Is he still *alive* and well somewhere? Or did his experiments go wrong, turning him into a creature that will haunt the White Mountains forever?

The Princess

Not all ghosts are scary. Some make it their purpose to care for the living.

Carolyn Foster, owner of the Mount Washington Hotel, always acted like royalty, and she treated her guests like royalty too. Then, in 1913, Carolyn actually *became* royalty when she married a French prince named Aymon Jean de Faucigny-Lucinge. After that, everyone called her the "Princess."

The Princess outdid everyone with her hospitality, elegance, and charm. Every evening when the guests met for dinner in the hotel's lovely dining room, Carolyn would glide through the room in her stunning dress, wowing everyone with her style and grace. When she traveled, she brought her own bed with her: a fancy, maple four-poster that had to be taken apart and put back together at every location.

Despite her appearance and the luxuries she enjoyed, Carolyn didn't act like she was better than others. The Princess was personable and kind, always making sure her guests were comfortable. Everyone loved her.

In 1936, Carolyn Foster died . . . but she didn't leave.

Ever since the Princess's death, guests and staff of her beloved Mount Washington Hotel (now renamed the Omni Mount Washington Resort) have reported odd sightings. Some people have seen the ghost of an elegant woman dressed in clothing from the early 1900s floating down the halls. Others have heard taps on their doors during the night, but when they answer, no one is there.

But it's the guests who stay in room 314 who report the most ghostly activity. Many have woken during the night to the strange sensation that someone is sitting on the end of their bed. Others have seen the Princess standing at the window brushing her hair. One family experienced the fireplace turning on by itself and belongings mysteriously disappearing only to reappear later in plain sight. Why does Carolyn visit this room more than all the others? The answer is simple. That's where her beloved maple four-poster bed is.

Although people are shocked at experiencing these supernatural events, no one feels afraid. They describe their encounters as "magical" and "peaceful." One guest told the staff that when she saw the Princess sitting on her bed, she wasn't scared. She felt a sense of calm, as if the Princess had just dropped by to make sure everything was okay.

How would you feel if you woke up to a ghost sitting on your bed? Would you feel comforted? So far, most guests at the hotel do, all thanks to the caring spirit of Carolyn Foster.

Paranormal Page-Turners

Imagine you're in Portsmouth, New Hampshire, taking a trip to the library.

You step out of the summer sun into the cool air and are enveloped by the smell of books and paper. You browse for a while, walking between the stacks, running your fingers lightly over spines, hovering on titles that tempt your curiosity.

Remembering that you have a project to work on, you head to the reference section.

While searching for books on your subject, you hear a shuffling sound and then footsteps coming from above. You look up at the balcony and glimpse the face of a curly-haired child who backs away out of view as soon as he's spotted.

Something about this doesn't seem right. What is an unattended child doing up there? "Hello?" you call. "Is anyone there?" There is no answer.

Finished with your reference text, you go to the Special Collections room to look for more information on your topic. There, you find the perfect book for your purpose. Excited, you say aloud, "Yes! This is just what I need."

"SHHH!" The hush is loud in your ear, and you jump, unaware that anyone was nearby. But when you turn around, no one is there. It's as if the shushing sound came from nowhere. A chill travels down your back, and you decide you've found enough resources for today.

You check out your books and exit the library. As you leave, you see a man crossing the street from the direction of the health food store. When he passes you, you get a funny feeling. On a hunch, you turn around and see him enter the library . . . by walking straight through a wall.

You've just met the three ghosts of the Portsmouth Public Library.

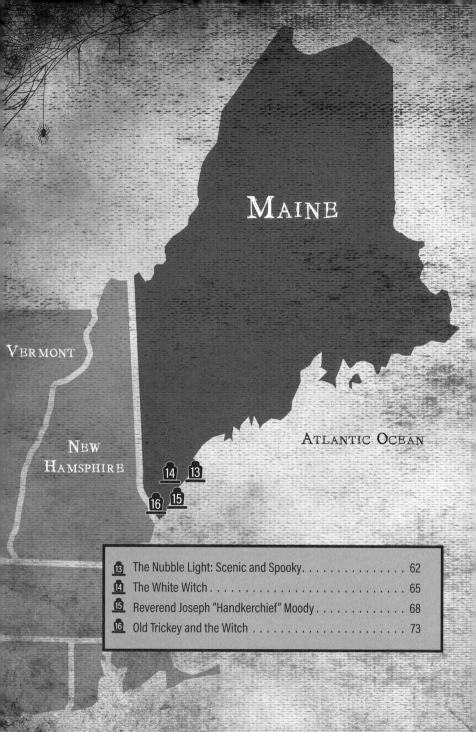

MAINE

VERMONT

NEW
HAMSPHIRE

ATLANTIC OCEAN

Maine

Lobsters, lighthouses, literary giants, and lively beaches. Maine is a tourist's dream with delicious food, beautiful ocean views, and diverse landscapes. But there is a sinister side to some of those lighthouses, and creepy characters from Maine's past still walk the earth in this most northern New England state. Let's meet some of them, shall we?

The Nubble Light: Scenic and Spooky

The Nubble Light in York, Maine, is the most photographed lighthouse in America. When you see it, you understand why. Located on a tiny rocky island less than two hundred feet from Nubble Point, the picturesque Nubble Light stands proudly next to a quaint white house with a pitched red roof and a white picket fence. On a clear day, it sits postcard-perfect between the brilliant blue sky and rich blue waves. The whole scene looks so inviting that it's difficult to imagine the little island having a dreadful and deadly past. But it does.

On Thanksgiving in 1842, years before the Nubble Lighthouse was built, a 396-ton ship called the *Isadore* left Kennebunk, Maine, for New Orleans, Louisiana.

Captain Leander Foss and his crew never made it to their destination.

Less than fifty miles into their journey, a severe storm blew in, ravaging the ship. The next morning, the wrecked remains of the *Isadore* washed up onshore, along with the bodies of Captain Foss and twelve crew members. The only surviving crewman of the ill-fated *Isadore* was Thomas King. The night before the ship set sail, Thomas had a dream that catastrophe awaited on the journey, so he did not board the vessel. He hid in the woods until his crewmates stopped looking for him. Thomas's dream saved his life.

For the rest of the *Isadore* crew, their untimely

demise rests heavy on their souls. Witnesses have reported seeing a phantom ship sail past the Nubble Light at night, with a crew of thirteen ghostly sailors staring forlornly out at the sea.

Although the tale of the *Isadore* is not a happy one, there is also a mysterious positive energy swirling around the Nubble Lighthouse. Many people who visit the light feel a comfort and inspiration similar to magic, and some claim that their visit to this beautiful New England landmark changed their lives for the better.

Where does this positive force come from? Maybe it stems from the beauty of the house next to the lighthouse. It looks as perfect as a dollhouse, and its gables act as a compass, helping pilots navigate from above. Or maybe the sense of peace comes from the light itself and the knowledge that, thanks to the Nubble Light, the York shore won't have to see a tragedy like the *Isadore* again.

CHAPTER 14

The White Witch

In a playground across from a cemetery in York, Maine, children squeal with delight as they play on the swings. "Higher!" they call, and Mary, the kind young woman they met at the park, pushes them harder. From afar, their mothers watch, foreheads creased in puzzlement, for there is no one with their children at the swings . . .

The people of York say there is nothing to worry about. The children have simply encountered the benevolent spirit of Mary Nasson, otherwise known as the White Witch.

Mary was born in 1745. She grew up in York Village and married Samuel Nasson. She was a well-known and respected herbalist in the town. (An herbalist, as you may imagine, is someone who knows how to use herbs to treat lots of illnesses and injuries.) She also knew how to perform exorcisms and helped multiple families clear their homes of the demons they felt were there. (Something that was pretty common back then.) Mary's ability to heal and her skills in dealing with evil entities earned her the nickname "the White Witch." Unfortunately, Mary had a very short life. She died when she was only twenty-nine years old, before she got the chance to become a mother.

The White Witch was laid to rest in Old Burying Yard, and her grave is very unique. Her portrait is carved into the top of her headstone, and a large granite slab was placed between her headstone and footstone. Originally, all the plots in the cemetery were covered like this to prevent livestock from disturbing the graves. Eventually a wall was built around the graveyard to keep the livestock out. The granite slabs were not needed anymore, so they were removed and used to line the top of the wall. All but Mary's. Her grave in the far corner of the cemetery is the only one still covered.

The White Witch's body may have left the world in 1774, but her spirit is still around. The crows that routinely visit the graveyard are supposedly her familiars, and Mary's ghost still roams the area, floating around her odd grave marker and playing with the children she never got to have. But nobody seems to mind. Everyone agrees Mary was one of the "good" witches. Some say that her gravestone is always warm to the touch, even on a cool day. Perhaps that's further proof that her benevolent spirit shines on.

Reverend Joseph "Handkerchief" Moody

The legend of Joseph Moody is a tragic one, full of sadness and guilt and judgment from beyond the grave.

In 1732, when he was thirty-one years old, Joseph Moody became the minister at the Second Church of York, Maine. Things went fine for a while, and the reverend was well-respected. Then, when his wife died suddenly, Moody fell into a severe depression. It is understandable to experience sorrow and grief when a loved one dies, so the parishioners were sympathetic with their pastor and gave him the time he needed to recover.

But when Reverend Moody came back to preach again, he did so with a black veil covering his face. This alarmed the congregation, who began to worry about the poor man's mental health. However, behind the veil the minister sounded sane of mind, even witty. His sermons were rational and thought-provoking. This made people think there must be another reason for the shroud—maybe the reverend was ill or suffering from a skin condition.

Still, despite the fact that his sermons were good, Reverend Moody's eerie appearance was too much for most people to bear. They began asking other ministers to perform weddings and preside over festive occasions. After all, who wants to be married to the love of your life by a man in a black veil?

The more people shunned Joseph Moody, the more he withdrew from society. He still gave sermons at church on Sunday, but he spent the rest of his time alone. At night, his gloomy figure could be seen roaming the shore or taking nightly walks through the cemetery—always behind the veil. People began calling him "Handkerchief" Moody and avoided him. Eventually, Moody stopped preaching altogether and became a total hermit. When his former parishioners glimpsed him through the window of his home, he was often seen sitting with the black veil over his face, staring at the wall.

"Handkerchief" Moody died in 1753 and was buried at Old Burying Yard with the veil over his face. At the time, his strange behavior was a mystery to those who knew him, but years later, the terrible truth came out.

Before Moody died, he asked a fellow minister to come to him so he could give his final confession. What Moody told the man made his blood run cold.

When Joseph was a young man, before he became a reverend, he went on a hunting trip with his best friend. Thinking he had a deer in his sights, Joseph squeezed the trigger and shot. It wasn't a deer. Joseph had accidentally killed his best friend. Overwhelmed with grief and terror and afraid of being arrested for the crime, the distraught boy made his friend's death look like an Indian attack. The trick worked. Everyone believed the poor young man had been murdered by Native Americans.

But Joseph was not okay. From that day

forward, the restless spirit of his best friend hovered in front of him always, insisting that he tell the truth about that awful day.

Eventually, the guilt of his terrible deed and the years of dishonesty were too much for Reverend Moody to bear. He decided no one should ever have to look upon his deceitful face again and covered himself with the veil to shield the world from his sins.

The reverend's shame and guilt followed him his whole life, tormenting him and sending him to an early grave. But it also provided literary inspiration. Intrigued by the life of "Handkerchief" Moody, famous New England author Nathaniel Hawthorne wrote a short story called "The Minister's Black Veil."

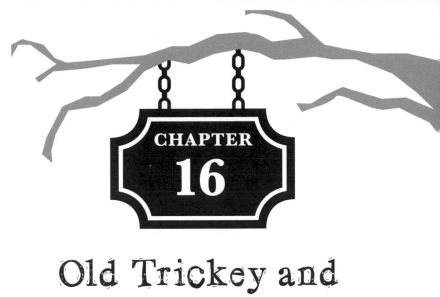

Old Trickey and the Witch

There are two more creepy characters you should watch out for if you visit Old York. Both of them made an impact on York in the 1700s, and their spirits linger just as much as their legacies.

There are two theories about the origins of William Trickey. Some say he was a cruel and vicious pirate, and people stayed away from him due to his wicked demeanor. Others claim that his shunning was because of a suspicion of witchery. They say that when Trickey arrived in the town, corn withered, crops failed, and sheep died.

Either way, the locals called him "Old Trickey." They say when he died, he was ushered into Hell by the devil himself, who sentenced Trickey to haul sand with a bucket on a rope for all eternity. Now, on stormy nights, the harbor howls with the tormented screams of Old Trickey, yelling for more rope and sand as he endlessly toils.

Old Trickey's Bible resides in the Old York Historical Society's archives. Witnesses say the holy book refuses to stay open and slams closed when anyone tries to read it.

The other sinister specter to steer clear of is the ghost of a woman executed for being a witch. The young woman, whose name time has forgotten, was hanged in front of the building that is now the York Historical Society Museum. But before she died, she put a curse on the town, swearing to come back to the spot where she was killed and haunt the inhabitants forever.

Now, objects move around at the museum, and doors open and close on their own. Visitors to the museum often feel icy blasts of air from unseen sources. Even outside the building, people encounter cold spots on warm days. If there were any doubt about who is to blame for these phenomena, the transparent apparition of the woman herself sometimes materializes in the spot where she was hanged. Is she trying to run people off? Or is she coming to make sure the people of York don't forget her—and the curse she placed on their town?

MASSACHUSETTS

CONNECTICUT

17
18   19

RHODE
ISLAND

ATLANTIC OCEAN

Connecticut

If you're looking for a state with a strong sense of American culture, look no farther than Connecticut. The fifth state to join the union, Connecticut's state song is "Yankee Doodle," and Mark Twain, the father of American literature, made his home here. One particularly magical part of Connecticut is Mystic. Here, history and modern charm collide in a variety of museums, restaurants, shops, and tourist attractions. But the magic of Mystic is *so* alluring, it's also attracted tourists from beyond the grave. Read on to learn where you can find these mysterious visitors.

CHAPTER 17

The Mysteries of Mystic Seaport

You've decided to visit Mystic Seaport, the largest museum of maritime history in the world. What an excellent decision! The sun is shining, the water is a deep blue, and people all around are enjoying the boats, shopping, and demonstrations. Here, you watch blacksmiths work metal at the forge. There, you see how rope is made. And farther away, visitors are lined up to tour the famous whaling ship, *Charles Morgan*. The whole scene is alive with activity. Only, it turns out, some of the guests here are *not* alive.

You choose to do a little shopping. First, you head to the variety store. The heavy door squeaks when you open it, and once you're inside, it closes with an audible thud. As you walk around, you pass a family shopping. You nod, but they don't return your greeting. Something feels odd about the family. You turn around for a second look, but they're gone. You search the whole store, but they are nowhere to be found. Maybe they just left, but wouldn't you have heard the squeak of the door and the heavy thud of it closing? A chill crawls up your spine as you realize the family was never there at all, not in *this* world anyway.

Next you visit the museum shop. This building used to be a private home, and some parts still look as they did more than a century ago. When you venture close to some shelves near the staircase, the air suddenly feels colder, and you get a creepy feeling in your gut. Something tells you to leave the area. You follow your instincts and turn around. A second later, you hear a crash. Whirling back around, you see glassware toppling off a shelf as if an invisible figure is mischievously sweeping their arm along the merchandise.

Deciding you've had enough shopping, you head to the Spouter Tavern for lunch. You've just taken a bite of your delicious sandwich when the lights flicker off and on. Then you hear the creak of footsteps in the rafters above you . . .

No one knows who the ghosts of Mystic Seaport are, but there's one thing visitors can agree on: when you're in Mystic Seaport, you're never alone.

Spectral Sailors Aboard the *Charles Morgan*

One of the most captivating attractions of Mystic Seaport is the *Charles Morgan*, an all-wooden whaling ship that first set sail in 1841. This 113-foot vessel rigged for 13,000 square feet of sail is a beautiful relic from the bygone days when America relied on whale oil to burn in lamps and to keep machinery greased and working.

Thankfully, civilization has found

replacements for whale oil, and the majestic sea creatures no longer need to be hunted. But in the mid-1800s, crews of thirty-five men would sometimes spend as long as five years aboard ships like the *Charles Morgan* in search of the valuable cargo.

Whaling was a dangerous job, and plenty of sailors lost their lives on duty, so it should come as no surprise that their souls sometimes haunt the ships where they breathed their last. The *Charles Morgan*, which retired in 1921 after thirty-seven voyages, certainly has a few.

If you take a tour of this famous boat, keep your eyes peeled for phantoms. One transparent sailor has been seen smoking a pipe below deck, and several staff members have heard mysterious voices floating up from the bunks and the sounds of footsteps when no one else was near. Some employees refuse to be alone on the *Charles Morgan*. In addition to hearing the strange noises, they've actually felt the cold touch of an invisible figure while aboard. Imagine feeling the grasp of a seafarer who died more than a hundred years ago! That's enough to give anyone the chills.

The *Charles Morgan* is considered the pride of Mystic Seaport, and it's worth a visit even if you don't see a ghost. But . . . you might.

The Haunted Emporium

For more than fifty years, a variety store called the Emporium sat at 15 Water Street, in Mystic, Connecticut. The store sold wacky gifts, unique toys, and creative crafts, but the strangest things in the Emporium were the ghosts.

One mischievous spirit that haunted the Emporium was that of a twelve-year-old boy. He liked to hang out in the store's toy section and play tricks on the female employees. But Becky, who used to be the assistant manager, learned how to handle him. She'd shout, "Don't freak me out today!", and the ghost would listen to her. It wasn't just staff who noticed the aura of the ghost boy, though. Customers also felt a presence in the toy section, and a few actually saw the apparition of a boy there.

Perhaps this young trickster was the same ghost who pestered the previous owner of the Emporium's site. Shortly after Paul bought the building, he was fixing it up when he literally painted himself into a corner. Not wanting to walk across the room's newly painted floors, he called to an assistant out the window asking for a ladder so he could climb out of the room that way. But when Paul turned back around, there was already a set of footprints ruining the fresh paint. No one else—no one living anyway—had entered the room.

The Emporium itself wasn't the only haunted spot in the building. Cindy, longtime manager of the variety store, lived upstairs for a number of years, and her apartment was also troubled with energy from the other side. No clock would ever work in her kitchen, and mysterious footsteps could sometimes be heard in that room. Cindy and her son felt a disturbing force in one particular doorway. They always scooted past that spot as quickly as possible. If they left the apartment for a couple of days, items fell off shelves, as if the entities were trying to tell them they didn't like being alone.

Despite the somewhat frightful events, Cindy never believed there was anything evil about the spirits lurking in her apartment or store, and she has a theory about why they might have been hanging around. She says the original purpose of the building was a post office during the Civil War. A lot of news from (and about) soldiers passed through the space, and not all of it was happy. Cindy thinks the energy in the building could have been left over grief from the bad news that exchanged hands there or from the loved ones still waiting to hear from their long-lost soldiers.

Unfortunately, the Emporium closed its doors in 2013, but the building remains at 15 Water Street. Who knows? Maybe the ghosts do, too.

MASSACHUSETTS

RHODE
ISLAND

CONNECTICUT

ATLANTIC OCEA

Rhode Island

Rhode Island may be small in square miles, but it's big in supernatural encounters. In fact, some say there are more ghosts in Newport, Rhode Island, than anywhere else in New England. So when you visit the Ocean State, keep your eyes and ears open for the pirate phantoms that wander the shore and the wailing wraiths whose voices still carry in the breeze.

CHAPTER 20

The Screaming Armor and Other Terrors of Belcourt Castle

There are certain things you expect to see when visiting a castle: ornate furniture, statues, a suit of armor. What you don't expect is furniture that throws you across the room, statues with spirits hovering around them, or suits of armor that scream. But that's what you'll find if you visit Belcourt Castle in Newport, Rhode Island.

Belcourt Castle was built in 1894. It was designed by Richard Morris Hunt, who also designed the base of the Statue of Liberty. Thomas Edison, the famous inventor, designed the castle's lighting. Belcourt Castle has sixty rooms and front doors so wide that the original owner, Oliver Hazard Perry Belmont, could drive his horse and carriage through them and right into his mansion.

The Belmonts passed away in the early 1900s, and the castle sat empty until 1956, when Harle and Donald Tinney bought it and fixed it up. They filled the grand house with family heirlooms and antiques, a few of which came with an unexpected "bonus."

One eerie object was a statue of a monk that stood near the grand staircase of the castle. Guests began seeing the ghost of a monk drifting down the staircase. Then, during a tour of the castle, the guide was talking to a group of visitors about the statue when several people gasped in shock. They'd just seen a phantom appear behind the guide! Concerned, the owners consulted a psychic who said if they moved the statue to the chapel, the monk's spirit would be at peace. Harle Tinney followed the woman's advice, and the ghost of the monk stopped making trouble.

The monk may have frightened some guests, but at least he never tried to hurt anyone. The same can't be said for a pair of chairs in the castle.

Yes, *chairs*.

If you visit Belcourt Castle, you may notice two antique chairs roped off in the ballroom. Tread carefully near these innocent-looking pieces of furniture because they give off a violent energy. It's well known that if you touch them, you will feel the blood drain from your fingers. One woman tried to sit on one, and an invisible force threw her across the room! No one knows what happened to give the chairs such negative energy. Whatever it was, it must have been terrible to cause such a long-lasting impact.

But the most famous haunted item in Belcourt Castle is neither a statue nor a chair. It's a suit of armor.

The Tinneys own several suits of armor. They are displayed in a row at the front of the ballroom. One suit seems to still be inhabited. Harle and Donald first noticed something was wrong when Harle walked past the ballroom one night and noticed the lights were on. When she went to investigate, she heard a scream. Frightened, she switched off the lights and turned to flee. That's when she heard a second scream and turned to find the lights were back on again. The terrified woman turned the lights off again and heard a *third* bloodcurdling scream that sent shivers down her spine. It came from one of the suits of armor!

Harle rushed off to find Donald, who brought their two rottweilers to investigate the sounds. But the dogs refused to enter the ballroom.

The owners were not the only ones to hear the screams. Virginia Smith, a tour guide at the castle, was locking up one day when she heard a deep, rasping moan coming from one of the suits of armor. While she stood there, frozen in terror, the moan grew into a horrifying shriek.

Since then, witnesses have heard the scream on multiple occasions. Sometimes, the suit of armor raises its right arm just before sounding its hair-raising screech.

What's the story behind these awful screams? The Tinneys have an idea. The suit of armor that wails has a hole in the back of its helmet that could have been made by a battle-axe. They believe the man who wore the armor was killed in battle and now is doomed to relive his terrible death forever.

If you ever find yourself in Newport, Rhode Island, make a visit to Belcourt Castle. Guests never know what they'll see—or hear—in this haunted building.

The Black Duck

Would you be comfortable staying at an inn named after a smuggler's ship, one whose crew died a violent death? Would you be able to turn the lights off in a place where phantom voices and footsteps are often heard? Would you sleep soundly knowing that once in that very hotel all the alarm clocks in every room went off at the same time? If the answer is yes, you need to take a trip to the Black Duck Inn in Newport, Rhode Island.

The Black Duck Inn was named after a famous boat that illegally transported alcohol during Prohibition. One foggy night in 1929, the Coast Guard had had enough of this vessel and its unlawful activity. They fired on the boat, killing three of the four members of the crew. This incident sparked an all-out war between bootleggers and the Coast Guard. There was more violence and much controversy over the event, leading to an investigation.

Perhaps it's the ghosts of the slain crew members who haunt the inn that bears the *Black Duck*'s name. Maybe not. But *someone* is there. Lights go on and off at odd times, and footsteps can be heard upstairs when no one is on the upper floor. Voices come from unoccupied rooms, and, as mentioned before, once every alarm clock in the inn went off at one time, distressing all the guests who hadn't set their alarms at all.

Mary Rolondo, who bought the Black Duck Inn in 1994, has witnessed these creepy phenomena herself. One year, just before Christmas, she was cleaning a room when she heard someone speaking nearby. She was alone in the inn. Mary told an interviewer, "I heard this low mumbling voice beside me. I froze . . . It then rose to an audible level, then faded away quickly." She couldn't understand the words the voice was saying, but Mary has no doubt that there was a presence from the other side with her that day. She's also heard the ghostly footsteps so

often she recognizes them and can tell them apart from other guests.

The original *Black Duck* left its mark on history, and now its namesake is doing the same. Stop in for a stay at this haunted inn and keep your ears open for ghostly voices. Maybe *you'll* understand what they're trying to tell us.

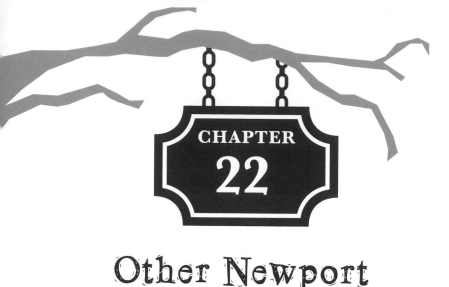

Other Newport Haunts

The ghosts of Belcourt Castle and the Black Duck Inn have plenty of friends in Newport, which may be the most haunted location in all of New England. If your goal is to visit all the creepiest places in the area, you won't want to miss these three . . . if you think you can handle them.

Fort Adams State Park is a great place to take in the scenery and the history of New England. Built in the mid-1800s and active through

World War II, Fort Adams is the largest coastal fortification in the United States. There's much to see during your visit, and they even host "youth overnights" where groups of students or Scouts sleep in the soldiers' actual barracks. But you might want to pack a flashlight and a little extra bravery if you choose to stay all night at Fort Adams, because visitors have seen strange shadowy movements and heard otherworldly voices during their stay.

Another haunted spot in Newport is Goat Island. On July 19, 1723, twenty-six pirates were hanged for their sea crimes at Gravelly Point. Then their bodies were buried on Goat Island. At night, when the moon shines its light on the small island, the pirate phantoms rise and roam the shore. They seem eager to get back to their ships, anxious to take revenge on their executioners.

Just outside of Newport, in neighboring

Middletown, is Purgatory Chasm. The chasm is a deep, narrow split in the rock along the seashore. This unique natural wonder was formed by glaciers thousands of years ago. The chasm grows each year, as seawater continues to erode the rock. The chasm is now 120 feet long, 10 feet wide at the top, and 150 feet deep. That's the height of a 15-story building!

Legend tells of a Native American woman who murdered a white man two hundred years ago. As punishment for her deed, the devil Hobomoko chopped off the woman's head and tossed her body into this deep, narrow chasm. Now, her headless spirit wanders the cliff edge where she met her end. So if you're ever near Purgatory Chasm at night, keep a look out for the headless woman . . . if you dare.

See? There's more to these scenic states than meets the eye. New England holds a special place in the heart of America and is home to remarkable residents of all types, both living and dead.